MW00904272

This book belongs to

_____

Activity Book Tips!

 Color with pencils, gel pens, or markers. Slip a piece of cardboard behind the page you're working on in case the markers bleed through.

 Take your time, be creative, and have pride in your work. Enjoy the time doing the activities rather than racing to finish.

Answers and solutions are in the back of the book.

A totally faedorable activity book for 4-8 year olds with fantasy, fairy, mermaid, unicorn, and dragon designs by Selina Fenech.

As an artist, color is a thing of magic in my life. Color creates shapes, forms, and feelings in the artworks I paint. Laying color onto a blank page is when I feel closest to true magic, when I feel happiest and most relaxed, and it's through what I create that I share my love of magic with the world. Through my coloring books I want to share that same magic with you.

Happy coloring! ~ Selina XOX

See more art and coloring fun at www.selinafenech.com

Totally Faedorable Activity Book by Selina Fenech
First Published April 2020 by Fairies and Fantasy PTY LTD
With thanks to K.A. Last www.kiladesigns.com.au
ISBN: 978-1-922390-05-9

Artworks Copyright © 2019 Selina Fenech. All rights reserved.
No part of this book may be reproduced in any form or by any electronic or mechanical means including information storage and retrieval systems, known now or hereafter invented, without permission in writing from the creator. The only exception is by a reviewer, who may share short excerpts in a review.

All About ME

NAME: _____   AGE: _____

My favourite

COLOR _____

FOOD _____

ANIMAL _____

MY FAMILY
_____

I'M REALLY GOOD AT:
_____

WHEN I GROW UP I WANT TO BE:
_____

I LIKE TO READ:
_____

Tea Party Maze

HELP THE DRAGON THROUGH THE MAZE
TO FIND HIS TEA CUP.

COLOR THIS PAGE
AFTER YOU'VE FOUND THE WAY.

START

FINISH

5

Spot the Difference

COMPARE THIS PICTURE TO THE ONE BELOW, THEN FIND AND CIRCLE SEVEN THINGS THAT ARE MISSING.

WHEN YOU HAVE FOUND ALL THE MISSING THINGS IN THE PICTURE ABOVE, COLOR THIS ONE IN.

Fantasy Beasts Word Search

BUNYIP	DRYAD	GARGOYLE	PEGASUS	SELKIE
CENTAUR	FAIRY	GRIFFIN	PHOENIX	UNICORN
DRAGON	FAWN	KRAKEN	SATYR	VAMPIRE

S	T	F	A	I	R	Y	D	K	I	O	P	L	O
E	F	A	A	H	J	L	D	R	A	G	O	N	P
L	G	W	S	D	T	F	C	X	Z	A	S	A	L
K	H	N	Z	C	E	N	T	A	U	R	X	I	D
I	J	A	G	Q	G	H	Y	C	D	G	S	V	F
E	I	S	R	K	L	O	P	Y	U	O	K	G	B
Q	U	N	I	C	O	R	N	A	V	Y	L	H	U
W	A	C	F	S	A	H	D	Z	X	L	S	Y	N
E	V	V	F	W	B	K	R	A	K	E	N	T	Y
D	A	F	I	X	N	G	Y	X	F	H	S	S	I
F	M	R	N	D	H	S	A	T	Y	R	A	W	P
G	P	E	A	R	D	D	D	F	G	Y	K	E	I
T	I	T	S	T	S	W	S	D	Y	U	H	Y	U
Y	R	S	C	G	H	J	P	H	O	E	N	I	X
P	E	G	A	S	U	S	L	K	H	U	J	I	O

Crack the Code

USE THE SYMBOLS TO PLACE THE LETTERS IN THE CORRECT ORDER AND CRACK THE CODE.

A — D — E — I — L — M

N — P — S — T — W

Color in Fun!

Tic-Tac-Toe

PLAY WITH A FRIEND AND TAKE TURNS WRITING O AND X. TRY TO GET THREE IN A ROW.

Decorate the Fairy

USE COLORED PENCILS, PENS, MARKERS, SEQUINS, WOOL, OR FABRIC TO DECORATE THE FAIRY.
LET YOUR IMAGINATION RUN WILD!

Find the Shadow

MATCH THE UNICORN TO THE CORRECT SHADOW THEN COLOR THIS PAGE.

1   2   3   4

Draw Nessy

USE THE GRID AS A GUIDE TO DRAW NESSY BELOW, THEN COLOR HIM IN.

Dots and Boxes

PLAY WITH A FRIEND. TAKE TURNS DRAWING A LINE FROM ONE DOT TO ANOTHER. IF THE LINE COMPLETES A SQUARE THAT PLAYER WRITES THEIR INITAL IN THE BOX THEN DRAWS ANOTHER LINE. THE PLAYER WITH THE MOST BOXES WINS.

PLAYER ONE

WINNER

PLAYER TWO

Count and Color

COUNT THE STARS THEN WRITE THE NUMBER IN THE BOX, COLOR THE PICTURE.

27

Fantasy Crossword

FIT THE WORDS INTO THE GRID BELOW. ONE HAS BEEN DONE FOR YOU TO GET YOU STARTED.
THEN COLOR THE PICTURE.

M E R M A I D

CASTLE
DRAGON
FAIRY
MAGIC
~~MERMAID~~
UNICORN

Jigsaw Puzzle

CUT ALONG THE DOTTED LINE TO REMOVE THIS PAGE FROM THE BOOK.
COLOR THE PICTURE THEN CUT OUT THE PIECES TO MAKE YOUR OWN PUZZLE.

Word Unscramble

USE THE PICTURES AS CLUES TO UNSCRAMBLE THESE WORDS,
THEN COLOR THE PAGE

CEPRSNIS

_ _ _ _ _ _ _ _

RIFAY

_ _ _ _ _

CIHWT

_ _ _ _ _

Finger Puppets

CUT ALONG THE DOTTED LINE TO REMOVE THIS PAGE FROM THE BOOK. COLOR THE UNICORNS THEN CAREFULLY CUT THEM OUT. CUT OUT THE PAPER STRIPS AND USE STICKY TAPE TO ATTACH THE STRIP TO THE BACK OF YOUR PUPPET, FORMING A LOOP TO FIT YOUR FINGER.

Fishy Friends

DRAW SOME MORE FISHY FRIENDS AROUND THE MERMAID
SO SHE CAN SHARE HER TEA WITH THEM. THEN COLOR THIS PAGE.

Puzzle

CUT OUT EACH SQUARE AND GLUE THEM TO THE PUZZLE TO FILL IN
THE MISSING PIECES, THEN COLOR THE PICTURE.

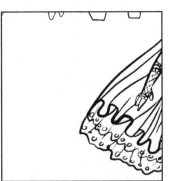

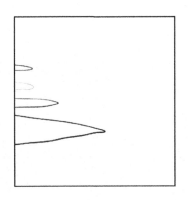

Write a Story

IF I WERE A MERMAID FOR A DAY, I WOULD ...

_____

_____

_____

_____

_____

_____

_____

_____

_____

Match the Pairs

Match the picture to its pair by placing the correct numbers in the boxes, then color this page.

Magical Maze

HELP THE WITCH THROUGH THE MAZE
TO FIND HER LOST KITTY.

COLOR THIS PAGE AFTER YOU'VE FOUND THE WAY.

START

FINISH

49

Spot the Difference

COMPARE THIS PICTURE TO THE ONE BELOW, THEN FIND AND CIRCLE FIVE THINGS THAT ARE MISSING.

←

WHEN YOU HAVE FOUND ALL THE MISSING THINGS IN THE PICTURE ABOVE, COLOR THIS ONE IN.

→

Color in Fun!

Fairy Tale Word Search

APPLE   MIRROR
CASTLE   PRINCE
CURSE   PRINCESS
FABLE   QUEEN
FAIRY TALE ROSE
KING   SLIPPER
MIDNIGHT   TOWER

P	R	I	N	C	E	S	S	Q	E	T	U	O	P
R	D	Z	A	Q	C	A	S	T	L	E	X	P	O
I	C	D	G	D	A	P	U	Y	T	V	F	Z	F
N	V	S	T	H	S	P	J	K	L	N	M	F	A
C	G	X	H	Y	D	L	A	R	S	A	Q	A	I
E	J	C	U	R	S	E	D	O	K	L	T	Y	R
A	M	Z	Y	U	G	D	F	S	P	O	H	M	Y
K	I	N	G	A	X	Q	U	E	E	N	G	Y	T
G	D	P	U	T	R	E	W	S	D	F	B	N	A
H	N	M	V	C	R	T	U	I	J	K	L	V	L
M	I	R	R	O	R	C	V	B	F	A	B	L	E
S	G	J	K	L	M	V	Y	U	I	V	D	S	E
Z	H	E	R	T	H	S	L	I	P	P	E	R	Z
X	T	O	W	E	R	G	H	W	E	Q	S	X	G

Crack the Code

USE THE SYMBOLS TO PLACE THE LETTERS IN THE CORRECT ORDER AND CRACK THE CODE.

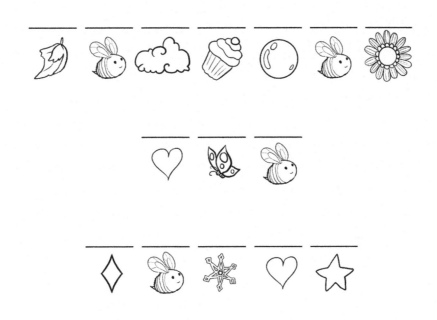

A   C   E   G   I   L

M   P   R   T   Y

Tic-Tac-Toe

PLAY WITH A FRIEND AND TAKE TURNS WRITING O AND X. TRY TO GET THREE IN A ROW.

Decorate the Tea Cups

USE COLORED PENCILS, PENS, MARKERS, SEQUINS, WOOL, OR FABRIC TO DECORATE THE FAIRY AND HER TEA CUPS AND SAUCERS. LET YOUR IMAGINATION RUN WILD!

Find the Shadow

MATCH THE FAIRY TO THE CORRECT SHADOW THEN COLOR THIS PAGE.

1   2   3   4

Draw the Cupcake

USE THE GRID AS A GUIDE TO DRAW THE CUPCAKE BELOW.

Dots and Boxes

PLAY WITH A FRIEND. TAKE TURNS DRAWING A LINE FROM ONE DOT TO ANOTHER. IF THE LINE COMPLETES A SQUARE THAT PLAYER WRITES THEIR INITAL IN THE BOX THEN DRAWS ANOTHER LINE. THE PLAYER WITH THE MOST BOXES WINS.

PLAYER ONE

WINNER

PLAYER TWO

Count and Color

COUNT THE BEANS THEN WRITE THE NUMBER IN THE BOX, COLOR THE PICTURE.

Magical Crossword

FIT THE WORDS INTO THE GRID BELOW. ONE HAS BEEN DONE FOR YOU TO GET YOU STARTED. THEN COLOR THE PICTURE.

| W | I | T | C | H |

BROOMSTICK

MAGIC

POTION

WAND

~~WITCH~~

WIZARD

Jigsaw Puzzle

COLOR THE PICTURE THEN CUT OUT THE PIECES TO MAKE YOUR OWN PUZZLE.

Word Unscramble

USE THE PICTURES AS CLUES TO UNSCRAMBLE THESE WORDS,
THEN COLOR THE PAGE

ANOGDR

_ _ _ _ _ _

ADIEMRM

_ _ _ _ _ _ _

RNOICUN

_ _ _ _ _ _ _

Finger Puppets

CUT ALONG THE DOTTED LINE TO REMOVE THIS PAGE FROM THE BOOK. COLOR THE DRAGONS THEN CAREFULLY CUT THEM OUT. CUT OUT THE PAPER STRIPS AND USE STICKY TAPE TO ATTACH THE STRIP TO THE BACK OF YOUR PUPPET, FORMING A LOOP TO FIT YOUR FINGER.

Color in Fun!

Sleep Tight

DRAW SOME MORE STARS AROUND THE ANGEL SO SHE CAN GET TO SLEEP.
THEN COLOR THIS PAGE.

Puzzle

CUT OUT EACH SQUARE AND GLUE THEM TO THE PUZZLE TO FILL IN THE MISSING PIECES, THEN COLOR THE PICTURE.

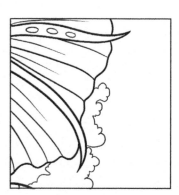

Write a Story

IF I WERE A FAIRY FOR A DAY, I WOULD ...

_____

_____

_____

_____

_____

_____

_____

_____

_____

_____

_____

Match the Pairs

MATCH THE PICTURE TO ITS PAIR BY PLACING THE CORRECT NUMBERS IN THE BOXES, THEN COLOR THIS PAGE.

Mermaid Maze

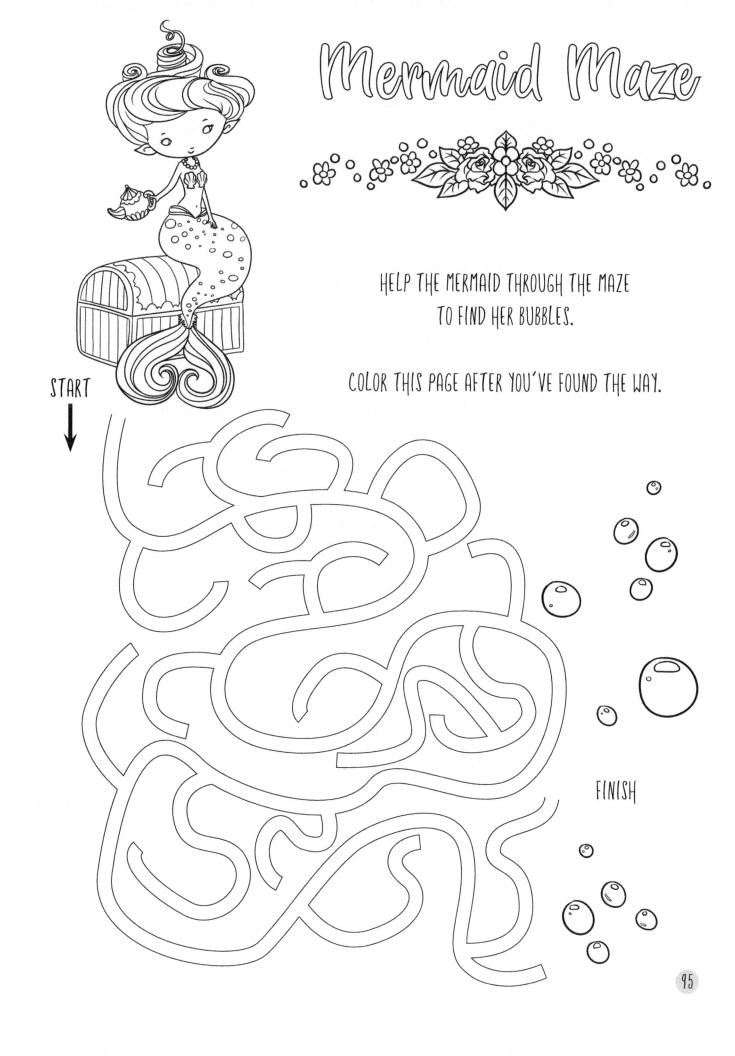

HELP THE MERMAID THROUGH THE MAZE
TO FIND HER BUBBLES.

COLOR THIS PAGE AFTER YOU'VE FOUND THE WAY.

START

FINISH

Fairy Word Search

BUTTERFLY   PIXIE
DAISY CHAIN   RAINBOW
ENCHANTED   SPARKLE
FAIRY RING   SPELLS
FLOWER   STAR
MAGIC   WAND
MUSHROOM   WINGS

A	F	G	W	I	N	G	S	Z	C	W	A	N	D
S	D	S	H	J	G	H	Y	T	R	D	S	A	A
B	U	T	T	E	R	F	L	Y	X	F	J	U	I
V	C	A	Q	N	S	A	K	V	C	X	J	K	S
C	S	R	Q	C	D	I	L	C	Z	A	S	L	Y
H	P	X	D	H	C	R	T	X	M	A	G	I	C
G	A	Q	J	A	K	Y	R	Z	K	L	A	D	H
J	R	K	V	N	S	R	Y	R	K	I	B	H	A
U	K	B	A	T	Q	I	D	A	L	T	Y	C	I
F	L	O	W	E	R	N	A	I	A	Q	R	T	N
K	E	S	C	D	A	G	W	N	P	I	X	I	E
I	D	F	G	U	H	R	T	B	L	B	C	Y	U
A	A	M	U	S	H	R	O	O	M	E	V	G	H
S	P	E	L	L	S	R	X	W	F	G	C	D	E

YOU WILL NEED:
PRINTER
PAPER/CARD
SCISSORS OR CRAFT KNIFE
6 PAPER FASTENER PINS

Instructions

1) CAREFULLY CUT ALONG THE DOTTED LINE TO REMOVE THE PAPER DOLL PATTERN PAGE FROM THIS BOOK. YOU MIGHT LIKE TO GLUE THE PAGE ONTO STURDY PAPER OR CARD SO YOUR DOLL WILL LAST LONGER.

2) COLOR IN THE DOLL BEFORE USING A SHARP PAIR OF SCISSORS OR A CRAFT KNIFE TO CUT CAREFULLY AROUND THE DOLL PIECES. ASK AN ADULT FOR HELP.

3) ATTACH THE LIMBS AND WINGS TO THE BODY USING SPLIT PIN PAPER FASTENERS, PINNING THROUGH THE SMALL BLACK DOTS. IF YOU HAVE USED THICK CARD, YOU MAY NEED TO POKE A HOLE WITH A CRAFT KNIFE FIRST. THE WINGS ATTACH BEHIND THE ARMS.

PRO TIP: PAPER FASTENERS COME IN DIFFERENT SIZES, CUTE SHAPES, AND COLORS! CHOOSE SOMETHING THAT MATCHES YOUR DOLL.

4) CAREFULLY CUT OUT THE SMALL SAMPLE DOLL AS A DOLLY FOR THE BIG PAPER DOLL.

5) SHARE A PHOTO OF YOUR PAPER DOLL ONLINE WITH #SELINAPAPERDOLLS

Paper Doll

Answers

PAGE 7

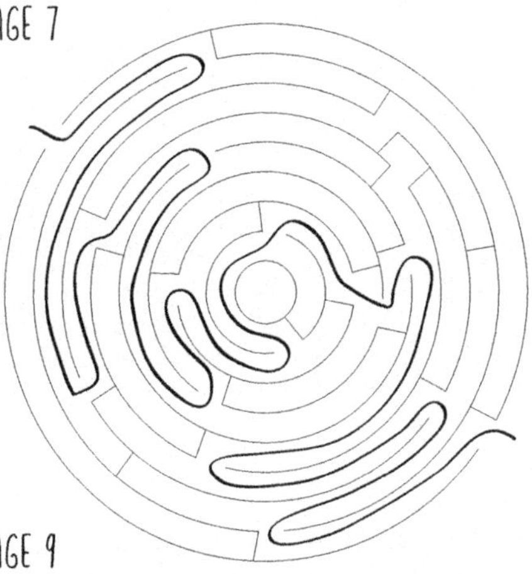

PAGE 9

PAGE 11

S	T	F	A	I	R	Y	D	K	I	O	P	L	O
E	F	A	A	H	J	L	D	R	A	G	O	N	P
L	G	W	S	D	T	F	C	X	Z	A	S	A	L
K	H	N	Z	C	E	N	T	A	U	R	X	I	D
I	J	A	G	Q	G	H	Y	C	D	G	S	V	F
E	I	S	R	K	L	O	P	Y	U	O	K	G	B
Q	U	N	I	C	O	R	N	A	V	Y	L	H	U
W	A	C	F	S	A	H	D	Z	X	L	S	Y	N
E	V	V	F	W	B	K	R	A	K	E	N	T	Y
D	A	F	I	X	N	G	Y	X	F	H	S	S	I
F	M	R	N	D	H	S	A	T	Y	R	A	W	P
G	P	E	A	R	D	D	D	F	G	Y	K	E	I
T	I	T	S	T	S	W	S	D	Y	U	H	Y	U
Y	R	S	C	G	H	J	P	H	O	E	N	I	X
P	E	G	A	S	U	S	L	K	H	U	J	I	O

PAGE 13: SWEET AND SIMPLE

PAGE 21: 3

PAGE 29: 30

PAGE 37: PRINCESS, FAIRY, WITCH

PAGE 49: 1, 4, 3, 2

PAGE 59: MAGICAL TEA PARTY

PAGE 67: 2

PAGE 73: 14

PAGE 81: DRAGON, MERMAID, UNICORN

PAGE 93: 2, 1, 4, 3

PAGE 31

PAGE 51

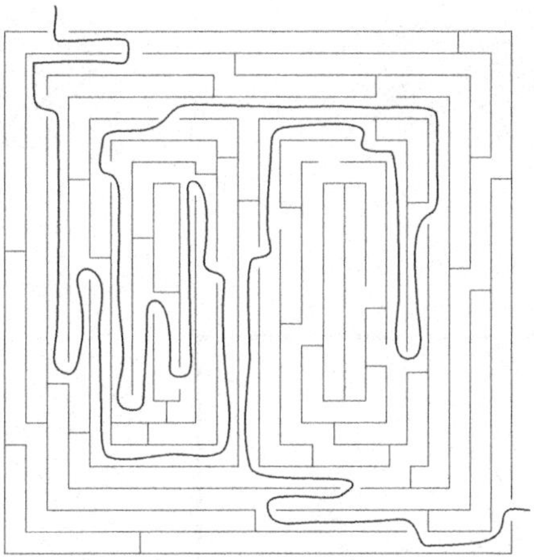

PAGE 53

PAGE 77

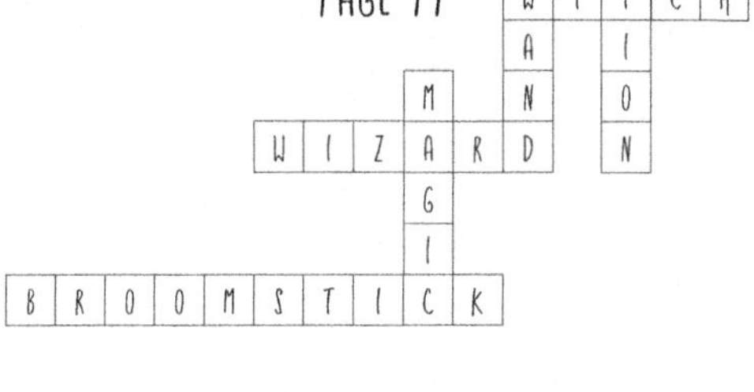

PAGE 57

P	R	I	N	C	E	S	S	Q	E	T	U	O	P
R	D	Z	A	Q	C	A	S	T	L	E	X	P	O
I	C	D	G	D	A	P	U	Y	T	V	F	Z	F
N	V	S	T	H	S	A	J	K	L	N	M	F	A
C	G	X	H	Y	D	L	A	R	S	A	Q	A	I
E	J	C	U	R	S	E	D	O	K	L	T	Y	R
A	M	Z	Y	U	G	D	F	S	P	O	H	M	Y
K	I	N	G	A	X	Q	U	E	E	N	G	Y	T
G	D	P	U	T	R	E	W	S	D	F	B	N	A
H	N	M	V	C	R	T	U	I	J	K	L	V	L
M	I	R	R	O	R	C	V	B	F	A	B	L	E
S	G	J	K	L	M	V	Y	U	I	V	D	S	E
Z	H	E	R	T	H	S	L	I	P	P	E	R	Z
X	T	O	W	E	R	G	H	W	E	Q	S	X	G

PAGE 97

PAGE 99

A	F	G	W	I	N	G	S	Z	C	W	A	N	D
S	D	S	H	J	G	H	Y	T	R	D	S	A	A
B	U	T	T	E	R	F	L	Y	X	F	J	U	I
V	C	A	Q	N	S	A	K	V	C	X	J	K	S
C	S	R	Q	C	D	I	L	C	Z	A	S	L	Y
H	P	X	D	H	C	R	T	X	M	A	G	I	C
G	A	Q	J	A	K	Y	R	Z	K	L	A	D	H
J	R	K	V	N	S	R	Y	R	K	I	B	H	A
U	K	B	A	T	Q	I	D	A	L	T	Y	C	I
F	L	O	W	E	R	N	A	I	A	Q	R	T	N
K	E	S	C	D	A	G	W	N	P	I	X	I	E
I	D	F	G	U	H	R	T	B	L	B	C	Y	U
A	A	M	U	S	H	R	O	O	M	E	V	G	H
S	P	E	L	L	S	R	X	W	F	G	C	D	E

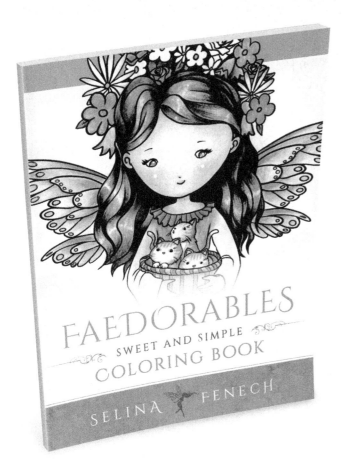

FAEDORABLES
SWEET AND SIMPLE
COLORING BOOK

SELINA FENECH

COLORING BOOKS

BY SELINA FENECH

So much more magic to color!

With over 100,000 copies sold, there are
more than 25 coloring titles to explore
your creativity through in Selina Fenech's
bestselling coloring range.

Themed signature range, Faedorables range,
pocket sized editions, grayscale editions,
coloring journals, and bundle collections.

Discover more at www.selinafenech.com

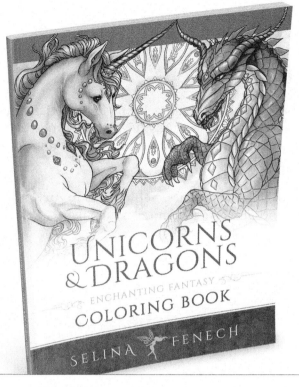

About the Artist

As a lover of all things fantasy, Selina has made a living as an artist since she was 23 years old selling her magical creations. Her works range from oil paintings to oracle decks, dolls to digital scrapbooking, plus Young Adult novels, jewelry, and coloring books.

Born in 1981 to Australian and Maltese parents, Selina lives in Australia with her husband, daughter, and growing urban farm menagerie.

Download printable coloring pages from all of Selina's coloring books at www.etsy.com/shop/printablefantasy

See all of Selina's bestselling coloring books, journals, art books and more at amazon.com/author/selina

Sneak a peek into Selina's studio and see what she's working on now at instagram.com/selinafenech/

Get social with Selina and see how others are coloring her work in her coloring group at bit.ly/colorselina

Made in the USA
Coppell, TX
27 March 2020

17794688R00063